Living the Catholic Social Tradition